UNPLUG WITH SCIENCE BUDDIES

MOVIN' AND SHAKIN' PROJECTS

Balloon Rockets, Dancing Pepper, and More

Rebecca Felix

Lerner Publications ◆ Minneapolis

Lerner Publications Company
A division of Lerner Publishing Group, Inc.
241 First Avenue North
Minneapolis, MN 55401 USA
For reading levels and more information, look up this title at www.lernerbooks.com.

Main body text set in Zemestro Std Book 12/16
Typeface provided by Monotype Imaging Inc.

Photo Acknowledgements
The images in this book are used with the permission of: Design elements and doodles © Artur Balytskyi/Shutterstock, © mhatzapa/Shutterstock, © Mighty Media, Inc., © Sashatigar/Shutterstock, © STILLFX/Shutterstock, © Tiwat K/Shutterstock, and © vesves/Shutterstock; © vasiliki/iStockphoto, p. 4 (kite); © Steve Debenport/iStockphoto, 5; © Motortion/iStockphoto, 6; © Mighty Media, Inc., pp. 7 (nails, balloons, aluminum foil, plastic bottle, Sharpies), 8–29 (project photos); © Nik Merkulov/Shutterstock, 7 (corks); © Laura Westlund/Independent Picture Service, p. 19 (whirlybird template); © Ranee Sornprasitt/iStockphoto, 30

Front and back covers: © Mighty Media, Inc.

Library of Congress Cataloging-in-Publication Data
Names: Felix, Rebecca, 1984– author.
Title: Movin' and shakin' projects : balloon rockets, dancing pepper, and more / Rebecca Felix.
Description: Minneapolis : Lerner Publications, [2020] | Series: Unplug with science buddies | Audience: Ages 7–11. | Audience: Grades 4 to 6. | Includes bibliographical references and index.
Identifiers: LCCN 2018058304 (print) | LCCN 2019003926 (ebook) | ISBN 9781541562455 (eb pdf) | ISBN 9781541554955 (lb : alk. paper) | ISBN 9781541574908 (pb : alk. paper)
Subjects: LCSH: Force and energy—Experiments—Juvenile literature. | Science—Experiments—Juvenile literature.
Classification: LCC QC73.4 (ebook) | LCC QC73.4 .F45 2020 (print) | DDC 531/.6078—dc23

LC record available at https://lccn.loc.gov/2018058304

Manufactured in the United States of America

Contents

Movement Unplugged

Have you ever seen a sailboat speed through the water? Or watched a hot-air balloon rise in the sky? These are examples of movement in action!

Technology has improved our use of movement to do work. This includes robots, drones, and remote-control toys. But the basic principles behind movement require no batteries or cords! From making floating pepper flakes dance to building a hot-air balloon out of a plastic bag, you can explore movement using household items and a little bit of science.

And the fun doesn't need to end once you've completed your project. Think of ways to experiment with your creation. What can you discover? Let's unplug and start making!

Before You Get Started

SUPPLY CHECK

Many of the projects in this book use common household items and craft supplies. These can include cotton balls, balloons, cups, and bowls. Other materials can be found at the grocery store, hardware store, or office supply store.

SAFETY FIRST

The projects in this book may require the use of sharp or hot objects. Ask an adult for permission before starting a project and request help when needed.

CLEANING UP

When you've completed a project, remember to clean up! Put supplies back where you found them, throw away garbage, wipe up spills, and wash dirty dishes. If you want to keep your creation, be sure to store it in a safe place!

AIR VORTEX

Create your own mini air cannons! Shoot swirls of air at toilet paper targets.

MATERIALS

- ☆ toilet paper
- ☆ tape
- ☆ measuring tape
- ☆ pen or pencil
- ☆ 8-ounce paper cup
- ☆ 16-ounce paper cup
- ☆ scissors
- ☆ 2 balloons

 ## SCIENCE TAKEAWAY

Pulling back and releasing the balloon creates a donut-shaped swirl of air. This is called a vortex. This shape is created because the air leaving the cup at the center of the hole is traveling faster than that leaving around the edge of the hole. The difference in air pressure between the fast-moving and the slow-moving air makes the vortex spin. This keeps the shape stable as it travels. The vortex travels through the air and moves the toilet paper.

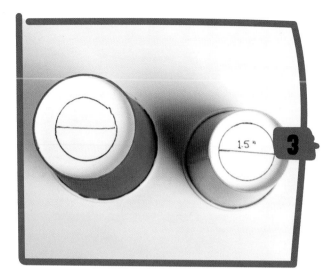

1 Have an adult help you tape several strips of toilet paper to the top of a doorframe. The bottoms of the strips should reach at least halfway to the floor.

2 Mark a spot on the floor 1 foot (0.3 m) from the doorway with a piece of tape. Mark another spot 3 feet (1 m) from the door and another spot 9 feet (3 m) from the door.

3 Draw a circle on the bottom of each cup. Make each circle 1.5 inches (4 cm) across. Have an adult help you cut out the circles.

4 Blow up the balloons to stretch them out. Let the air out of the balloons.

5 Tie the neck of each balloon in a knot. Cut about 0.5 inches (1.25 cm) off the other end of each balloon.

6 Stretch each balloon over the top of a cup. Tape each balloon to its cup all along the edge. This creates an airtight seal.

7 Stand on the 1-foot (0.3 m) mark. Aim the bottom of the small cup toward the toilet paper strips. Pull the balloon's knot back and release it. What happens?

8 Repeat step 7 from the other two marks. Then repeat again with the large cup. What happens?

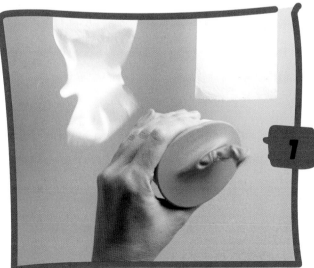

BALANCING ACT

Use everyday materials to create a mini balance beam. Explore how mass and gravity interact!

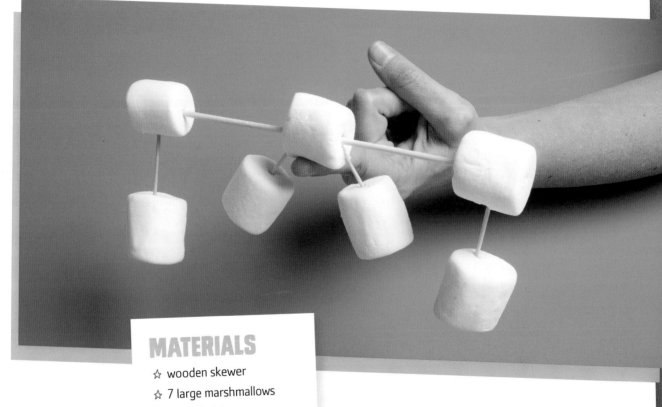

MATERIALS

☆ wooden skewer
☆ 7 large marshmallows
☆ 4 toothpicks

SCIENCE TAKEAWAY

Balancing a structure has to do with its center of mass. The marshmallow structure's center of mass shifts each time marshmallows are added. This makes the structure easier or more difficult to balance. The final version is easiest to balance because the bottom marshmallows lower the center of mass to right below your finger.

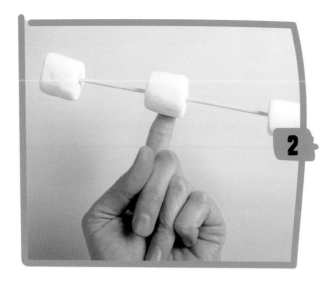

1 Push a skewer through a marshmallow until the marshmallow is in the center. Stick a marshmallow onto each end of the skewer.

2 Try to balance the structure on your finger. If it tips, move the center marshmallow slightly toward the end that tips up. Keep adjusting the center marshmallow until balancing the structure is easy.

3 Push a toothpick into each end marshmallow. Make sure the toothpicks point the same direction. Stick a marshmallow onto each toothpick.

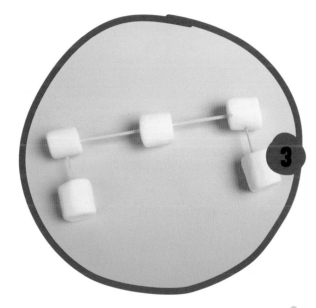

4 Try to balance the structure on your finger again. Is balancing it easier or more difficult than before? If necessary, adjust the middle marshmallow until balancing the structure is easy.

5 Push two toothpicks into the center marshmallow. Stick a marshmallow onto each toothpick.

6 Try to balance the structure on your finger again. Is balancing it easier or more difficult than before?

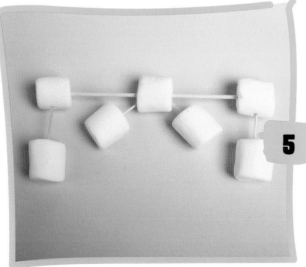

DANCING PEPPER

Experiment with surface tension to make pepper flakes dart across water!

MATERIALS

- ☆ shallow bowl
- ☆ water
- ☆ ground black pepper
- ☆ measuring spoons
- ☆ toothpicks
- ☆ cooking oil
- ☆ liquid dish soap
- ☆ milk
- ☆ toothpaste
- ☆ glass cleaner

SCIENCE TAKEAWAY

Water molecules stick to each other, creating surface tension. The surface tension is strong enough to act like a shell holding the pepper on the water's surface. Some liquids can decrease surface tension. When this happens, the water molecules move away from the areas with less surface tension, taking the pepper with them!

1 Fill the bowl about two-thirds full of water. Sprinkle 1 teaspoon of pepper over the water.

2 Dip the end of a toothpick in cooking oil and then into the water. Watch how the pepper behaves.

3 Empty and rinse the bowl. Repeat step 1.

4 Dip a clean toothpick in dish soap and then into the water. Watch how the pepper behaves.

5 Empty and rinse the bowl. Repeat the activity with the other household liquids. Watch how the pepper behaves with each one. Did they all have the same effect?

PARACHUTE RACE

Explore air resistance
with plastic parachutes!

MATERIALS

- ☆ garbage bags
- ☆ ruler
- ☆ scissors
- ☆ string
- ☆ 4 washers
- ☆ 4 twist ties
- ☆ high location, such as a balcony or playground platform
- ☆ stopwatch
- ☆ paper
- ☆ pen or pencil
- ☆ calculator

SCIENCE TAKEAWAY

Gravity pulls falling objects toward Earth. At the same time, air resistance pushes them up, slowing their fall. The larger parachute has more surface area than the smaller parachute. So, it has more air resistance and falls more slowly than the smaller parachute.

1 Cut two squares out of the garbage bags. Make the squares these dimensions:
8 × 8 inches (20 × 20 cm)
20 × 20 inches (51 × 51 cm)

2 The squares are your two parachutes. Tie a knot in each corner of both parachutes.

3 Cut eight 16-inch (41 cm) pieces of string. Tie the end of one string around each knot on the parachutes.

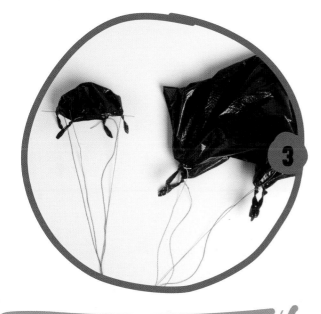

4 Pinch the center of a parachute. Hold it up so its strings hang down. Gather the ends of the strings together and tie them in a knot. Repeat with the other parachute.

5 Use twist ties to attach two washers to the ends of each parachute's strings.

6 Have an adult help you find a safe, high location from which you can drop the parachutes. Drop each one three times. Use the stopwatch to time each fall. Write down how long it took.

7 Add the three times for each parachute together. Then divide each total by three. This calculates each parachute's average falling time. Review your data. Which parachute fell fastest?

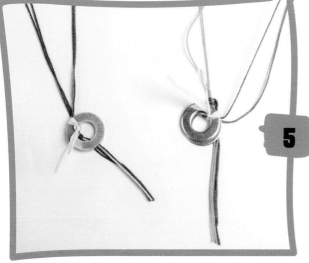

BOAT FLOAT

Learn how resistance and balance help boats move through water!

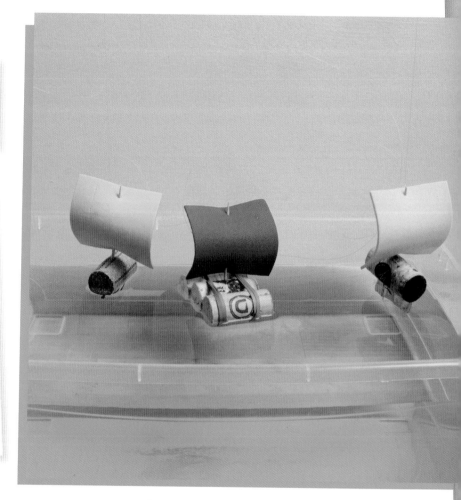

MATERIALS

- ☆ 5 corks
- ☆ rubber bands
- ☆ toothpicks
- ☆ craft foam
- ☆ ruler
- ☆ scissors
- ☆ small plastic tub
- ☆ water
- ☆ nails
- ☆ aluminum foil

SCIENCE TAKEAWAY

The large sailboat is the most stable. At first, the second boat is unstable and tips over. Adding a keel lowers the boat's center of mass, stabilizing it. However, the nails don't push through the water very well. This makes it hard for the boat to move straight. Adding aluminum foil to the third boat's keel gives the keel a fin shape. This cuts through the water, allowing the boat to move straight. This is how real sailboats work too!

1 Wrap two rubber bands around three corks. Push a toothpick into the center cork. The toothpick is the boat's mast.

2 Cut three squares out of craft foam. Make them each 2.5 inches (6 cm) on each side. These are sails.

3 Poke the mast through a sail near one edge. Slide the sail down to the corks. Bend the sail to poke the mast through the opposite edge.

4 Fill a small tub with water. Place the boat on the water. Blow on the sail. Watch how the boat moves.

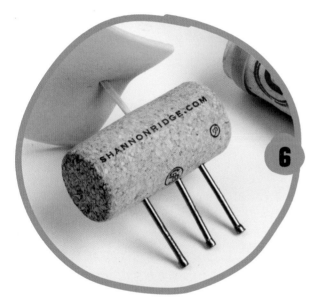

5 Push a toothpick into another cork. Repeat step 3 to add a sail. Place this boat in the water. What happens?

6 Remove the smaller boat from the water. Have an adult help you stick nails in a row along the bottom of the cork. This is a keel. Place the boat in the water. Add more nails as needed to keep the boat from tipping over.

7 Blow on the sail of the smaller boat. Watch how the boat moves.

8 Make another one-cork boat with a keel. Wrap aluminum foil around the keel.

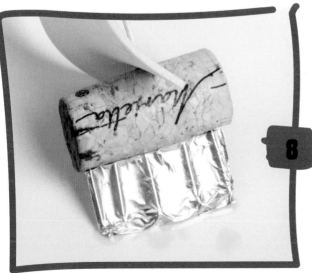

9 Place the third boat in the water and blow on its sail. Which boat moves straightest? Which moves fastest?

17

PAPER WHIRLYBIRD

Learn how lift battles gravity with a fluttering whirlybird!

MATERIALS

- ☆ paper
- ☆ ruler
- ☆ pencil
- ☆ red marker
- ☆ black marker
- ☆ scissors
- ☆ chair or stool
- ☆ stopwatch
- ☆ paper clips

SCIENCE TAKEAWAY

The whirlybird falls because gravity pulls objects toward the Earth. But the whirlybird blades create lift. Lift helps objects oppose gravity and fall more slowly. Adding paper clips increases the whirlybird's mass. The more mass an object has, the more gravity pulls on it. Gravity's pull increases but lift does not, so the whirlybird falls faster.

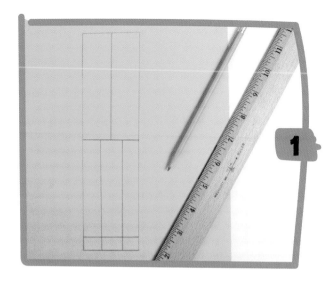

1 Copy the template below on a sheet of paper. Be sure to match the dimensions in the template.

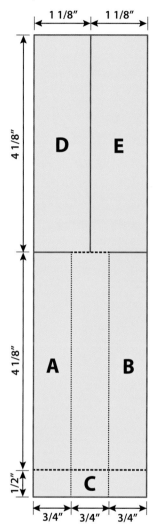

Template dimensions: 1 1/8" and 1 1/8" across the top; 4 1/8" for sections D and E; 4 1/8" for sections A and B; 1/2" for section C; 3/4", 3/4", 3/4" across the bottom.

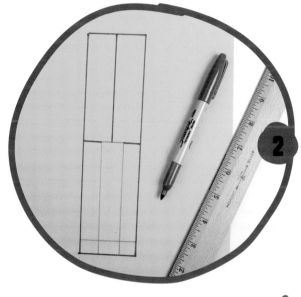

2 Where the solid lines appear in the template, trace the copy you drew in red.

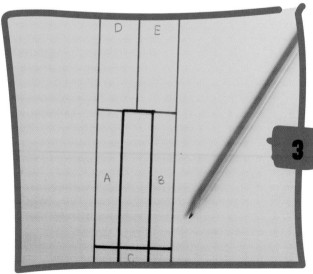

3 Where dotted lines appear in the template, trace the copy you drew in black. Add the letters so your copy matches the template.

Paper Whirlybird continued on next page

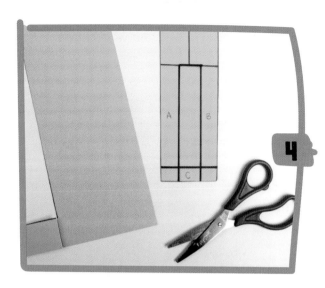

4 Cut along the red lines. Do not cut the black lines!

5 Fold part A toward part B. Fold part B over part A. Fold part C up. This creates a tab that holds A and B in place.

6 Fold part D down.

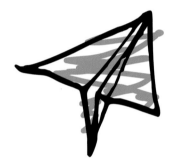

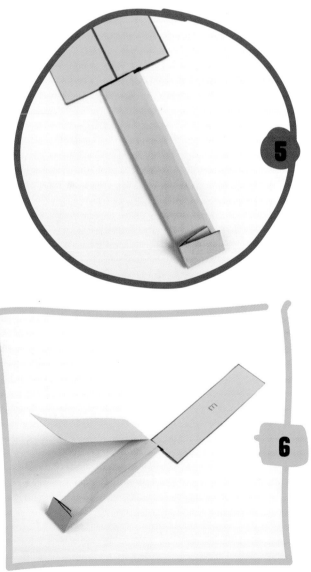

7 Fold part E back. Your whirlybird is complete!

8 Have an adult help you stand on a chair or stool. Drop the whirlybird. Drop it a few more times, observing how the whirlybird falls. Use the stopwatch to time how long it takes the whirlybird to hit the floor. Record the times.

9 Attach a paper clip to the bottom of the whirlybird. Drop the whirlybird again. What happens?

10 Add more paper clips to the whirlybird and drop it again. Did the added mass change how fast the whirlybird fell?

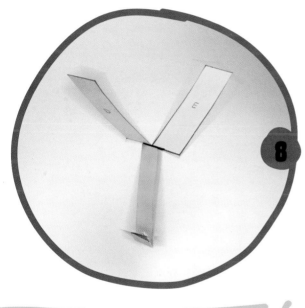

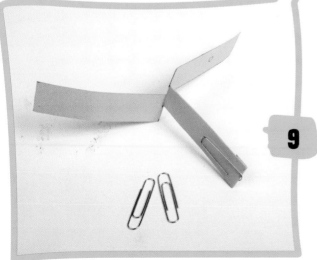

BALLOON ROCKET

Learn how mass affects speed with a rocket powered by balloon fuel tanks!

MATERIALS

☆ ball of string
☆ drinking straws
☆ 2 dining chairs
☆ scissors
☆ paper towel tube
☆ 2 modeling balloons (the long, skinny type used to make balloon animals)
☆ 2 binder clips
☆ tape

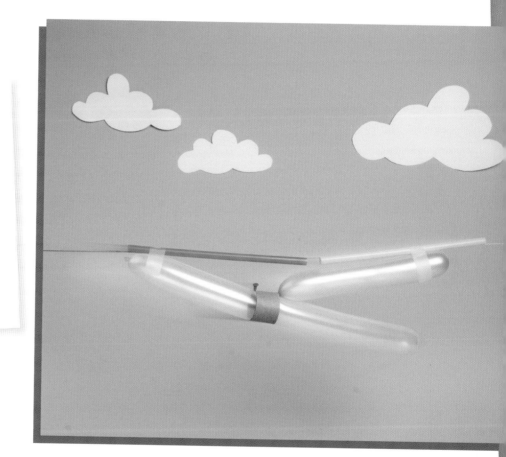

SCIENCE TAKEAWAY

Pressurized air inside an inflated balloon has energy. When this energy is released, it propels the balloon. Engineers create rockets that release energy in stages. Emptied fuel tanks break away, reducing a rocket's mass. This means less energy is required to keep the rocket moving. In your rocket, air is the fuel. Once the first balloon falls away, the resulting reduced mass allows the second balloon to go farther faster!

1 Place the two chairs at least 10 feet (3 m) apart.

2 Thread the end of the string through two straws.

3 Tie one end of the string to one of the chairs. Run the string to the other chair. Cut the string and tie the end to the second chair. Make sure the string is pulled tight and level between the two chairs. The two straws should be on the string between the chairs.

4 Cut a small ring from the paper towel tube.

5 Put one of the balloons through the cardboard ring. Inflate the balloon until its sides barely touch the inside of the ring. Twist the neck and use a binder clip to keep the air in. Do not tie the neck in a knot!

Balloon Rocket continued on next page

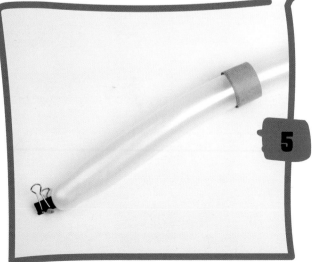

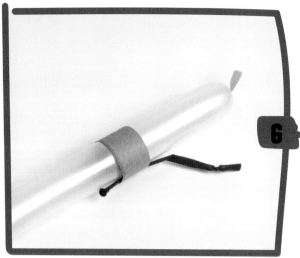

6 Carefully thread the second balloon through the cardboard ring in the same direction as the first. The neck of the balloon should be near the ring.

7 Inflate the second balloon. Twist the neck and use a binder clip to keep the air in.

8 Prepare for step 9! The goal of step 9 is to further inflate the first balloon until it is tight enough in the cardboard ring to keep the second balloon's end shut without using the binder clip. This can be tricky and take practice. Have an adult ready to help if necessary!

9 Pinch the end of the first balloon to hold it closed. Remove the clip. Inflate the balloon more and clamp it shut again. Carefully remove the clip from the second balloon. If no air escapes, move on to step 10. If air escapes from the second balloon, repeat steps 6 through 9 until no air escapes from the second balloon when you remove its clip.

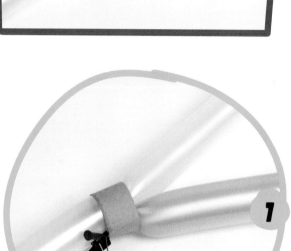

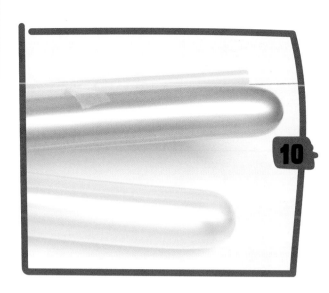

10 Tape each of the balloons to a drinking straw on the string.

11 Pull the clipped end of the first balloon to the chair at one end of the string. The other end of the balloon should face the other chair. Quickly remove the binder clip. What happens?

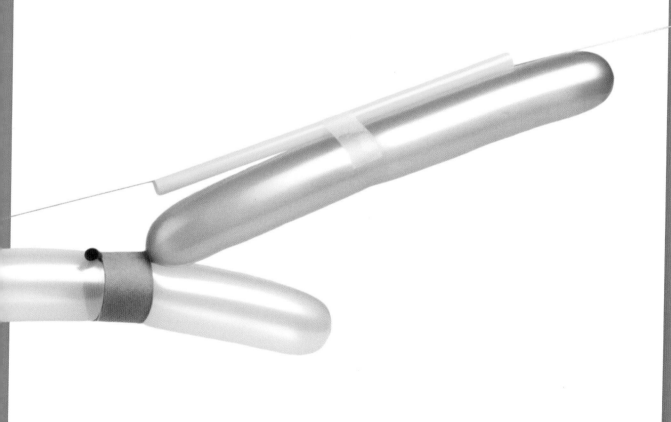

HOMEMADE HOT-AIR BALLOON

Explore how heat from a toaster can turn a plastic bag into a hot-air balloon!

MATERIALS

- ☆ toaster
- ☆ poster board, 3 × 2 feet (0.9 × 0.6 m)
- ☆ scissors
- ☆ tape
- ☆ ruler
- ☆ dry-cleaning bag
- ☆ sticky notes
- ☆ stopwatch
- ☆ notebook
- ☆ pen or pencil

SCIENCE TAKEAWAY

As air heats up, it expands and becomes lighter. This is how hot-air balloons fly. Air inside the balloon is heated and expands, pushing cooler air out. Once enough of the heavier cool air is replaced with lighter hot air, the balloon floats. The balloon material must also be lightweight for the hot air to be able to lift it upward.

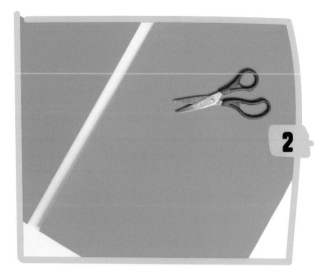

1   Make sure the toaster is unplugged. Clean out the toaster to remove crumbs. Set it up in an area with a high ceiling and no wind. Place the toaster on a clean, dry, and flat surface. With the supervision of an adult, plug in the toaster.

2   Fold the poster board in half lengthwise. Cut along the fold.

3   Tape the pieces of poster board together to make a long strip.

4   Wrap the strip around the toaster. Make sure there is about 2 inches (5 cm) of space between the poster board and the toaster. Tape the ends of the strip together to make a ring.

Homemade Hot-Air Balloon
continued on next page

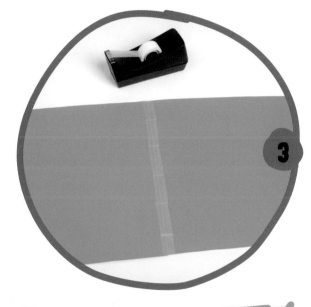

5 Examine the dry-cleaning bag. Cut off any extra plastic, such as shoulder corners. Be careful not to cut holes in the bag.

6 With the supervision of an adult, turn on the toaster. Place the dry-cleaning bag over the toaster and poster board ring. Hold the bag in place above the toaster as it begins to take shape from the hot air. Be careful not to melt the bag. If the bag tips and hot air escapes, use sticky notes to stick the bag to the surface. When the bag fills with enough hot air, it will pull the sticky notes up as well.

7 When the bag has filled with air, let go of it and start the stopwatch. Stop the stopwatch when the bag falls back down. Write down how long it flew.

8 Repeat steps 6 and 7 twice more. Was the flight time about the same each time?

9 Cut the bag in half to make it shorter. Repeat steps 6 through 8. Did the shorter length of the bag affect its flight time?

Explore More!

What fun movement projects did you complete? What did you learn as you experimented? Science is all around us, even when we aren't plugged into technology. And the more we experiment with science, the more we discover. So keep finding new ways to explore movement unplugged!

FURTHER INFORMATION

For more information and projects, visit Science Buddies at https://www.sciencebuddies.org/.

Ives, Rob. *Fun Experiments with Forces and Motion: Hovercrafts, Rockets, and More*. Minneapolis: Hungry Tomato, 2018.

Kingloff, Amanda. *Project Kid: Crafts that Go! 60 Imaginative Projects that Fly, Sail, Race, and Dive*. New York: Artisan, 2016.

Swanson, Jennifer. *Explore Forces and Motion! With 25 Great Projects*. White River Junction, VT: Nomad Press, 2016.

Glossary

air resistance: the force of air pushing on a moving object

center of mass: the point in an object or structure where an equal amount of mass is on each side

gravity: the force by which all objects in the universe are attracted to one another

keel: a long, heavy piece of wood or metal that is attached to the bottom of a ship

lift: the upward force that acts on a flying object

molecule: the smallest piece a material can be divided into without changing how it behaves. Molecules must be made up of two or more atoms.

pressurized: to be pressed tightly into a space or container

vortex: a whirling mass of air or fluid that creates a vacuum in the center that sucks things in

Index